TEARS IN THE JUNGLE

A CHILDREN'S ADVENTURE TO SAVE THE ORANGUTAN

Title:	Tears In The Jungle: A Childrens Adventure To Save The Orangutan
Authors:	Daniel Clarke & William Clarke
Photos:	Penny & Rodney Clarke
Dick Smith photo:	Pip Smith
Edited:	Maria Greenwood, Fiona Mitchell
Design and Layout:	Rodney & Penny Clarke
Target Audience:	Ages 3 to 15
Subjects:	Orangutan--Conservation--Juvenile literature. Orangutan--Conservation--Indonesia--Sumatra--Juvenile literature. Orangutan--Habitat--Conservation--Indonesia--Sumatra--Juvenile literature. Orangutan--Conservation--Borneo--Juvenile literature. Orangutan--Habitat--Conservation--Borneo--Juvenile literature.
Dewey Number:	599.883
Published by:	CTQ Management Consulting trading as Tears In The Jungle ABN 61 129 135 968 / BN98579264 PO Box 135 Terrey Hills NSW 2084, Australia info@TearsInTheJungle.com www.TearsInTheJungle.com
Printed by:	Ligare Pty Ltd, Sydney

FSC
www.fsc.org
MIX
Paper from
responsible sources
FSC® C011613

This book is dedicated to
our mum and dad for all their love and support.

Foreword

People have said to me it must have taken a lot of courage to fly around the world in a helicopter. But I can honestly say that my exploits are nothing compared to the courage shown by Daniel Clarke and his younger brother William.

I have known the Clarke family for some time, and their adventures are truly inspiring to me, and I believe to many others.

As they show so clearly in this wonderful book, the Clarke brothers have been deeply touched by their encounters with Borneo's endangered orangutans. Their campaign to save these wonderful animals and their habitat has moved many hearts, and I congratulate them for their wonderful efforts.

As you will see, it has not always been easy to travel along wild rivers or enter deep jungles, but the Clarkes rise to the challenge. I hope their adventures will move you as they have me, and I encourage you to join in their efforts to preserve some of the earth's most magnificent creatures.

Their spirit of adventure and determination to help others is a wonderful example to all of us.

Dick Smith

Dick Smith AO
Australian Adventurer
Explorer and Entrepreneur

Our names are Daniel and William Clarke and this is the story of our adventure through the jungles of Borneo, Indonesia, to learn more about orangutans, and their struggle for survival.

Nothing will stop us helping these beautiful animals and we hope that by sharing our story, you will join our quest to save them from extinction.

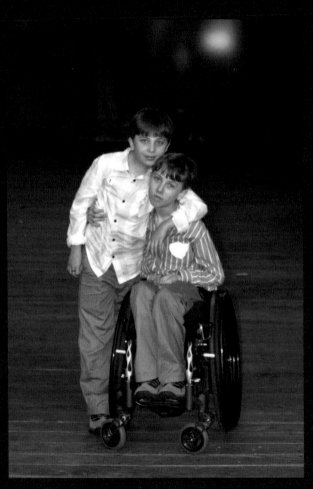

William Clarke (10) and Daniel Clarke (12)

In this picture Daniel is sitting in his wheelchair, as he has cerebral palsy and is unable to walk.

We live in Australia and we want to share our experiences we had with the orangutans, with other children, to help them to understand the problems and dangers they are facing.

We believe we can all work together to save the orangutans and their habitat in Borneo and Sumatra.

In total, our journey from Sydney (Australia) to Borneo (Indonesia) took two and a half days.

First we flew to Bali, then on to Jakarta. Here we took another plane to Pangkalanbun, Borneo, where our orangutan adventure began.

In Borneo, a bus picked us up from the airport and drove us to the port town of Kumai. We swapped our bus for a boat and travelled up the Kumai and Sekonyer River towards Tanjung Puting National Park.

Sumatra

Borneo

Australia

It was exciting travelling up river in the boat. The local people call these boats Klotoks because of the sound made by their motors.

The temperature during the day reached 38°C (100°F). It was very hot because Borneo is situated on the Equator. Thankfully for us, the river cooled the air a little.

The top deck of the Klotok was a great spot to sit and watch the jungle as we floated past. The bottom deck had places to sleep overnight and a small kitchen to prepare food. A very friendly lady cooked breakfast and lunch for everyone on the boat. She was a great cook. She even made deep fried bananas... Yum!

Do you know what was really funny?

You had to make sure that it wasn't raining before you went to the bathroom. The toilet at the back of the boat didn't have a roof!

We searched every tall tree along the Sekonyer River, hoping to see an orangutan or orangutan nest.

We didn't have to wait long…

Soon we spotted an orangutan nest high in a tree. It was amazing to see just how high the orangutans had climbed to make their nest.

FUN FACT

Orangutans build a nest in a different tree every night. Also, they don't like to get wet, so they collect branches and leaves to cover themselves if it's raining.

The jungle became thicker as we travelled up the river.
Our excitement grew - soon we would get to see our first
orangutan!

That evening we stayed at Rimba Lodge.
This was our base from where we travelled each day into the jungle.

Rimba Lodge is an eco-lodge where visitors from around the world can come and stay to see the orangutans in the wild.

The lodge is built on elevated walkways as it is next to the river. The walkways connect all parts of the lodge, making it easy to get around.

Our room at the lodge

The Dining Room

FUN FACT
An eco-lodge (or ecological lodge) is a hotel that tries to cause no or little damage to the surrounding animals, plants and land.

There is a troop of Long Tailed Macaques that live around the lodge. The dining room has lattice instead of windows to stop the monkeys coming in and taking food while you are eating.

Life at the lodge starts early.   Every morning the whole jungle wakes up at five in the morning. It was great to wake up and hear all of the birds and animals getting up at the same time. We could even hear the gibbons close by.

At the Tanjung Puting National Park, we caught up with our guides, who would stay with us for the rest of our journey.

They taught us all about orangutans and the jungle, and even how to say a few words and sentences in Indonesian.

The guides helped us carry Daniel and his wheelchair through the jungle so that we could see the local orangutans in their environment.

The orangutans watched and followed us as we walked through the jungle, swinging from branch to branch.

FUN FACT
Orangutans are arboreal. This means they live in trees.

Suddenly our guides pointed up into the trees. Right above us was the dominant male orangutan of the area. He was huge!

He was so heavy that branches fell from the trees everywhere he went. We had to be careful that they did not hit us on the head.

One of the females was curious and moved closer to us. She was smaller than the male and was able to climb between trees without breaking any branches.

We turned a corner to arrive at a feeding platform.

Each week, the orangutans come to this feeding platform to eat bananas which are brought by the guides. This feeding supplements their natural diet, while they learn to find their own food.

One banana

Two bananas

Too many bananas!

This orangutan made everyone laugh by seeing how many bananas he could fit into his mouth before climbing back up the tree. The guides said that the orangutans love bananas so much they take as many as they can from the feeding platform.

How many bananas is this orangutan trying to take away in one mouthful?

The next day, we continued travelling up the Sekonyer River, heading for Camp Leakey. The river was becoming narrower due to the dense rainforest.

Natural tannins from the leaves made the water a clear, dark reddish-brown.

Further upstream, gold mining had polluted the river, changing it to a cloudy, light brown colour.

The sign in the image reads:

Welcome to   Selamat Datang di

Camp Leakey

Established in 1971 by   Didirikan pada tahun 1971 oleh

Dr. Birute Mary Galdikas & Rod Brindamour

Funded by   Dana didukukung oleh

Orangutan Foundation International (OFI)

A non-governmental organization &   Sebuah
registered charity   Lembaga Swadaya Masyarakat

For more information please visit   Informasi lebih lanjut website kami
our website

www.orangutan.org

Orangutan Foundation   Pemkab KOBAR   Departemen Kehutanan

Mohon Jangan :
- Memberi Makan / Minum
- Makan / Minum Di Depan
- Menyentuh Orangutan

Peringatan : Jangan Menceb
Berenang Di Sungai Ada Buaya

Mohon Bawalah Sampah Anda
Bersama Anda   Terima Kasih

Please Do Not :
- Feed The Orangutans
- Eat In Front Of The Orangutans
- Touch The Orangutans

Warning : Do Not Swim In The R
There Are Lots Of Crocodiles

Please Take Your Litter With

www.orangutan.org

We finally arrived at Camp Leakey after travelling along the river for 2 ½ hours. Dr Birute Galdikas established Camp Leakey in 1971 and has been researching and working with orangutans in the wild ever since.

The camp has many orangutans that come and go whenever they like. Many of these orangutans were previously cared for at Camp Leakey, but were rehabilitated and released into the protected area of the national park after they had learned how to take care of themselves.

At Camp Leakey we came across a Gibbon, called 'Bob', just hanging around outside the laundry room.

The laundry room was secured with wire to prevent the gibbons and orangutans from playing with the clothes.

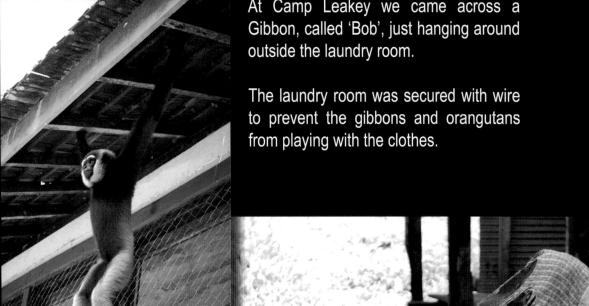

Just behind the laundry room we found Siswi, a 35 year old orangutan, playing with someone's shirt, now full of holes!

We watched Siswi for a while.

She found a comb in the dirt and knew exactly what to do with it. She started combing her hair on the top of her head.

Siswi was making herself beautiful!

Our guides explained how orangutans learn by watching and mimicking their human carers.

They are very intelligent.

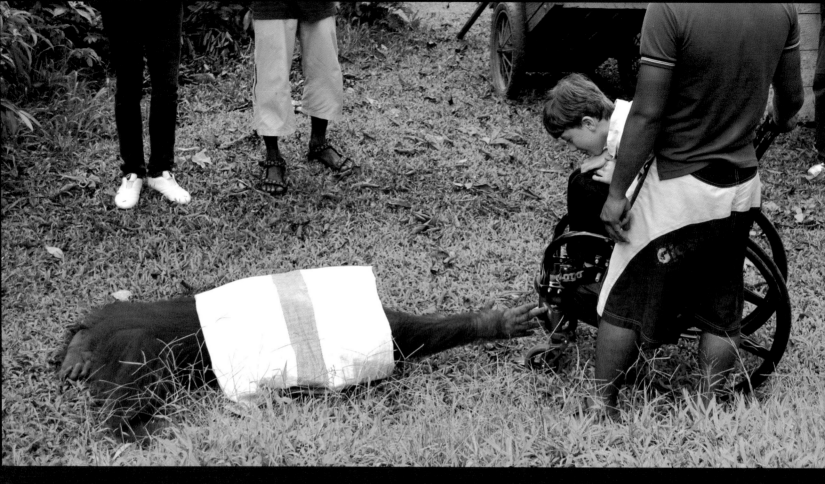

Orangutans are very curious. Siswi found a sack on the ground and put it over her head, pretending that no one could see her.

When Siswi saw Daniel's wheelchair, she wanted to play with it and pulled Daniel closer and closer.

Siswi was facinated with the wheels and even tried to let the air out of the tyres

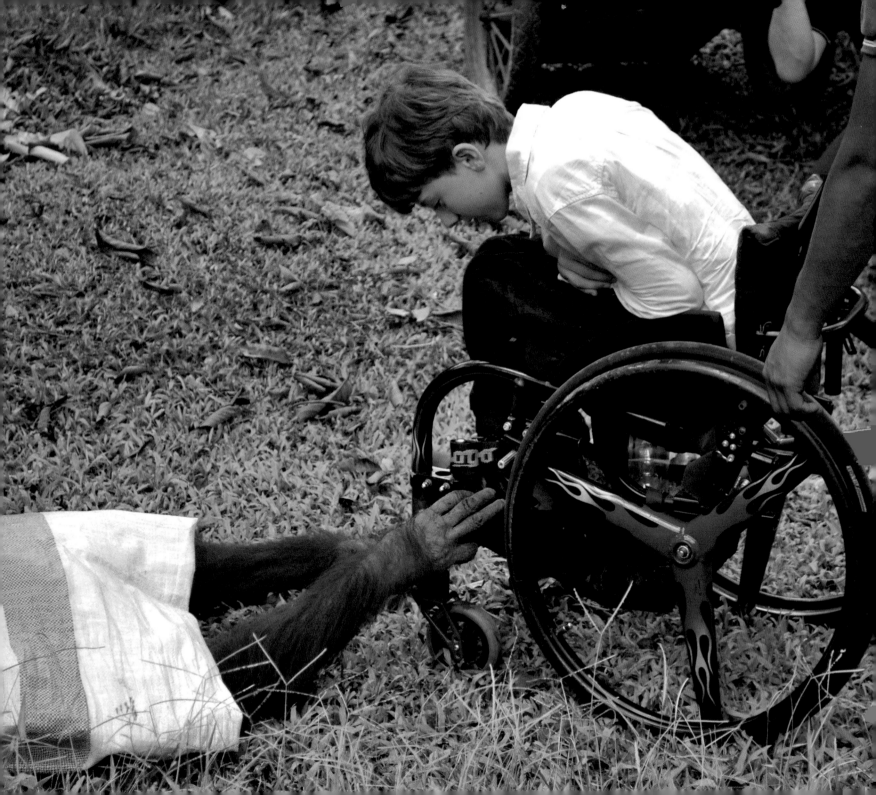

Siswi took her sack and climbed into the tree above us.

She started picking fruit, called Rambutan, and putting them into her sack - just as we would do if we were collecting fruit.

Rambutans are one of the favourite fruits of orangutans and grow throughout the jungles of Borneo.

Siswi was having so much fun, she looked like she was laughing.

FUN FACT
Orangutans use the same expressions and gestures as humans when they are happy and appear to be laughing - only without sounds.

After watching the orangutans at Camp Leakey, we went back to the boat to have some lunch, and Siswi decided to follow us.

Our guides gave her some juicy berries to eat so that we could spend time with her on the wharf, next to our boat.

Siswi sat with William.

She was so gentle and even copied his expressions.

"There is no better feeling than being able to communicate with an orangutan without speaking", William said.

Sitting with Siswi on the wharf was an amazing experience for both of us.

William felt honoured that Siswi wanted to hold his hand.

A large male, called Uranus,
came and sat next to Siswi
on the walkway by the wharf.

We were amazed to see how similar the hands of an orangutan look to those of a human. Their fingers and fingernails, in fact everything about them, were just like ours.

Uranus

The next day, we went back to watch the orangutans at the feeding platform. A female came down with her baby clinging tightly to her back. The baby was so cute.

As we walked back to the rangers' hut, another female joined us with her baby. Her name was 'Princess'. She is quite famous because she learnt sign language from her carer when she was very young.

She is now about 36 years old and still remembers how to communicate using sign language.

Hornbill

Long Tailed Macaque

Proboscis Monkey

Borneo has a large variety of jungle plants and animals.

On our walks through the jungle, we saw Proboscis monkeys, Macaques and Hornbills (an endangered bird). On the ground there were pitcher plants and ants the size of your thumb!

We also saw a family of Proboscis monkeys in a tree. They were all wet from swimming across the river.

Long Tailed Macaque

Ants the size of your thumb!

Pitcher plant

After our stay in the jungle, we went to an orangutan care centre.

Most of the orangutans at the centre are orphans, (they don't have a mother to look after them).

Baby orangutans are rescued daily from surrounding palm plantations. Farmers kill orangutans that wander into their plantations looking for food.

Logging of the jungle, and the development of palm plantations are destroying their habitat, and sources of food for the orangutans. If the farmers kill a mother with a baby, they try to sell the baby or keep it as a pet.

This is really tragic, as a baby orangutan needs to stay with its mother for at least the first seven years of its life. During this time the mother teaches the baby all the skills of the jungle.

When the babies arrive at the care centre, they are looked after by human carers. These carers teach them the survival skills their mothers would have taught them in the wild.

It takes the babies seven years to learn these important skills, just as if they were still with their mothers.

We were given special privileges to hold some of the babies who were between three and eight months old. They were so cute and just wanted to hug us.

It was also so sad.

We realised that these babies didn't have their mothers to look after them anymore.

All the babies live together at the care centre. Their human carers stay with them twenty four hours a day. They even sleep in the same huts with them at night.

As the babies get older (6-7 years) the men at the centre look after them, as they get too big and strong for the women to manage.

All of these orangutans spend six hours at jungle school each day.

At jungle school they are taught how to climb trees, find fruit to eat and to be aware of snakes.

One of the baby orangutans gave Daniel a very special hug.

"They are so beautiful, we have to save them!", said Daniel.

FUN FACT

Every orangutan is as individual as any one of us. They each have a unique hairstyle and facial expression. You can easily tell the difference between each one.

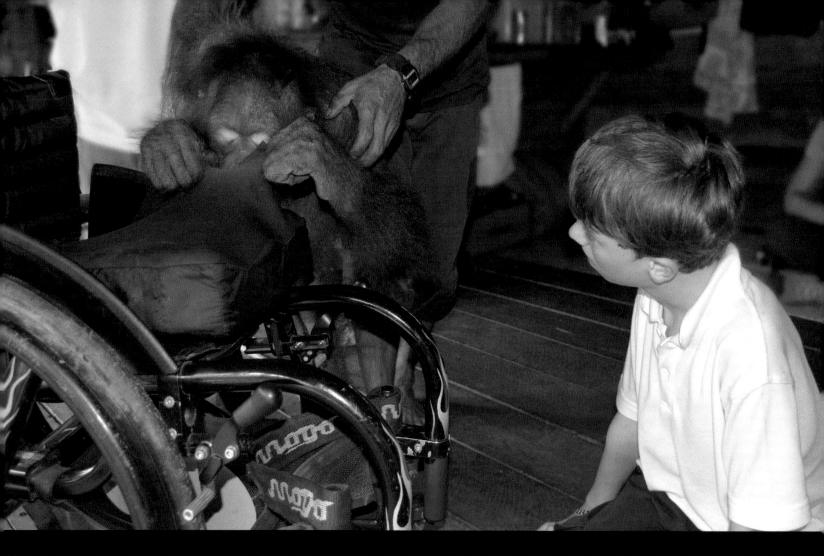

We learned so much about orangutans from the carers at the centre. It was fantastic to spend time with all of the orangutans we had adopted.

The orangutans were so curious about Daniel's wheelchair. One young female orangutan thought there may be some food in Daniel's seat, and tried to look underneath it. The carers said that this was the first time these orangutans had ever seen a wheelchair.

We watched the seven year old orangutans at school learning the skills of the jungle. As soon as we arrived the orangutans became very excited and wanted to show off.

They climbed up and down the small trees around us and even sat in Daniel's wheelchair.

They played with us as though we were young orangutans - just like them!

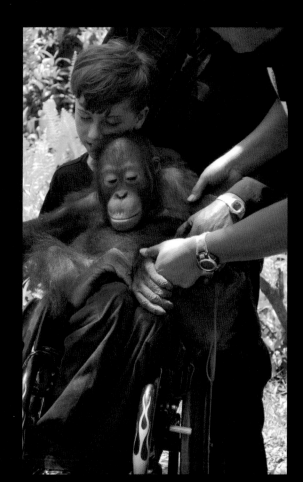

When the orangutans go to jungle school the carers let them explore and show them trees they can climb to find fruit.

The carers also teach them how to make nests and how to use twigs and branches as tools - everything their mothers would have shown them in the wild.

The orangutans were so playful especially one of the younger males. He tried to swing on William's arms as though he was a tree.

He loved to be tickled. It was just like playing with a little brother.

It was very hot in the jungle and everyone was very thirsty, even the orangutans. He really wanted some of William's water.

William poured some water into his hat, and then used his hat to pour the water into the orangutans mouth. He loved the water dripping over his head and made sure he caught every last drop.

The orangutans love to be with their carers, as well as being able to go into the jungle on their own.

They never go too far - just like a human baby would not wander too far away from their mother.

Their expressions were so funny. You knew exactly what they were thinking. This orangutan wanted to play with everybody's shoes.

They were very cheeky and naughty, but in a playful way!

This was the last day we would spend with the orangutans in Borneo. The trip had gone by so fast - we really didn't want it to end!

As we flew over Borneo on our way home, we could see the damage to the jungle from the air.

The valuable rainforest is being cleared by logging and setting fires to make room for palm plantations that produce palm oil for the rest of the world.

It was devastating to see the loss of orangutan habitat.

"Where are the orangutans going to live if we keep destroying their habitat?", asked Daniel.

We felt very sad saying goodbye to everyone, especially the orangutans.

It has been an incredible journey.

Daniel and William continue to
raise funds and awareness
to protect the orangutan
and its habitat.

For more information on their progress go to
www.TearsInTheJungle.com

ORANGUTAN FACTS

Scientific name	Pongo Pygmaeus (Borneo) Pongo Abeli (Sumatra)
Habitat	Orangutans live high in the trees of the jungle. They can only be found in Indonesia (Sumatra and Borneo) and Malaysia.
Weight	Adult male orangutans weigh up to 136 kg (300 lbs), while the females can weigh up to 50 kg (110 lbs).
Arm span	2 metres (7 feet)
Diet	Orangutans are frugivorous, which means they only eat fruit.
Birth	The female orangutan has one baby every nine years.
Life Span	Orangutans can live up to 40-55 years in the wild and 50-60 years in captivity.

DID YOU KNOW?

1. In Malay, the word 'orangutan' means 'person of the forest'.
2. Orangutans share 97% of our DNA.
3. The female orangutan only has one baby every nine years.
4. An orangutan baby stays with its mother for seven years.
5. Orangutans make a new nest every night, in a different tree.
6. Orangutans are arboreal, which means they live in trees.
7. Orangutans are frugivorous, which means they only eat fruit. When fruit is scarce, however, they will eat other foods such as bark, leaves and termites.
8. Orangutans are an important part of the eco-system because they spread the seeds from the fruit they eat around the forest.
9. There is a difference between the Sumatran and Bornean orangutans. Sumatran orangutans have long thick red hair while the Bornean orangutans have short dark brown hair.
10. Orangutans have prehensile feet, meaning that they can hold onto things with their toes. This is why they can climb trees so easily. Their big toes are like thumbs.
11. Orangutans can catch the same diseases as humans such as Malaria and the common cold.
12. The main visible difference between an orangutan (ape) and a monkey is that an ape does not have a tail.
13. A male orangutan develops cheek pads only when he is a teenager and is the only dominant male in the area.
14. An adult male orangutan has the strength of ten men.
15. Orangutans don't like the rain, so they make 'umbrellas' out of leaves.
16. Orangutans are very intelligent. They use sticks, leaves and bark as tools to reach for food.
17. Orangutans have a unique hair style, face and personality.
18. They are peaceful and friendly creatures.

THE MOST IMPORTANT THING WE CAN DO TO
SAVE THE ORANGUTANS FROM EXTINCTION IS SAVE THEIR HABITAT.

YOU CAN SAVE THE ORANGUTAN

The following organisations have orangutan programs that are focussed at rehabilitating and releasing orangutans back into the wild as well as protecting their habitat:

Australian Orangutan Project
www.orangutan.org.au

Borneo Orangutan Survival (BOS) Australia
www.orangutans.com.au

Sumatran Orangutan Conservation Program
www.sumatranorangutan.org

YOU CAN HELP CHILDREN, LIKE DANIEL, WHO HAVE ATHETOID CEREBRAL PALSY

To assist children with Athetoid Cerebral Palsy please make your donation at:

The Daniel Clarke Foundation
www.DanielClarkeFoundation.org.au

PO Box 135
Terrey Hills NSW 2084
Australia

THANK YOU

Thank you to our family and friends for supporting us in our quest:

Mum and Dad, Stephen Van Mil, Kobe Steele, Bruce Gardner,
Vicki Carter, Zed and George Holman, Terry Tisdale and Denise Walsh
and a special thank you to Dick Smith.

*For further information on Daniel and William's quest
to save the great apes of the world,
or to order further copies of their book,
go to www.TearsInTheJungle.com.*

*If you would like to get in contact with
Daniel and William you can email them at:*

Daniel@TearsInTheJungle.com   *William@TearsInTheJungle.com*